The Night Guard at the Wilberforce Hotel

Johns Hopkins: Poetry and Fiction

John T. Irwin, *General Editor*

The Night Guard at the Wilberforce Hotel

Poems by Daniel Anderson

Johns Hopkins University Press   Baltimore

This book has been brought to publication with the generous assistance of the Albert Dowling Trust and the Writing Seminars Publication Fund.

Printed in the United States of America on acid-free paper
9 8 7 6 5 4 3 2 1

Johns Hopkins University Press
2715 North Charles Street
Baltimore, Maryland 21218-4363
www.press.jhu.edu

Library of Congress Cataloging-in-Publication Data
Anderson, Daniel, 1964–
[Poems. Selections]
The Night Guard at the Wilberforce Hotel : Poems / by Daniel Anderson.
pages cm.—(Johns Hopkins: Poetry and Fiction)
ISBN 978-1-4214-1347-1 (Paperback : acid-free paper)—ISBN 1-4214-1347-7 (Paperback : acid-free paper)—ISBN 978-1-4214-1348-8 (Electronic)—ISBN 1-4214-1348-5 (Electronic)
I. Title.
PS3551.N3584A6 2014
811'.54—dc23 2013032889

A catalog record for this book is available from the British Library.

Special discounts are available for bulk purchases of this book. For more information, please contact Special Sales at 410-516-6936 or specialsales @press.jhu.edu.

Johns Hopkins University Press uses environmentally friendly book materials, including recycled text paper that is composed of at least 30 percent post-consumer waste, whenever possible.

For Jo and for my brother Geoff

Scout Tower Rock

Contents

I The Night Guard at the Wilberforce Hotel 3
Pardon and Amnesty 5
Almost 8
In Vino Veritas 11
From Here to There 15
Epithalamion in a Minor Key 18
At Advent's End 21

II This First Hot Saturday in May 27
A Late Apology 29
Provinces 31
Teaching *The Merchant of Venice* 34
The Hills, Beautiful Hills 37
Insomnia at Forty-Six 40
Easter Sundays 42

III Labor Day 47
The Novelist to His Characters 49
Someone Is Burning Leaves 51
Four Voices for the Afterlife 54
Mare Cognitum 60
Now: A Benediction 62

Acknowledgments 65

I

The Night Guard at the Wilberforce Hotel

The drunks on seventeen,
three San Antonio conventioneers,
snoggle at long last in their clean beds.
A naked man on five
has woken to the latch and click
of someone's lock, only it's his,
and clear as Christmas crystal there he is,
dream-dazzled in the hall,
not even so much as a shower cap
to hide behind. A guest
on twelve is calling to complain
about the Indiana newlyweds
whose bucking headboard batters at her wall.
They've heard it also on the floor below,
that beastly thumping racket,
as if the whole ceiling could cave in,
like something horrifying out of Poe.
But for the moment he has paused
over a pleated mound of towels,
a chilled, half-eaten omelet on a plate,
and cigarette stubbed in the last
flat, golden ounce of champagne in a flute
outside room 728.
He listens as a woman cries
and all at once it's 1954.
That was Kenosha. He is ten.

A sleepless, bathrobed little boy
studying the thin strip
of butter-colored lamplight
underneath his mother's bedroom door.
Though it's been more than fifty years,
it is her quiet weeping that he hears
as an old radiator knocks
and whistles at the cold.
Then he is jostled by
an elevator bell
or just the hoarse, pea-gravel sound
of someone making ice.
Regardless, he has gone
almost as softly as he first appeared
back to the handsome, chandeliered
and polished marble lobby, where
the night clerk and the married concierge
flirt purely out of boredom's sake.
Those rising and those still awake
look out on cargo ships
inching through metal-colored lanes
across the rain-strafed lake.

Pardon and Amnesty

A month ago
ice faceted the willow. Our first
forsythia and daffodils were stunned

beneath a pellet glaze of sleet.
And for a raw few days the punk
of winter fires reclaimed our dismal street.

But other flowers now are freshly sunned,
flamingo-pink azaleas and the rose.
A dust of violets blurs the college lawn,

and all these creamy dogwoods,
having tousled out of bud,
enjoy a dry, delicious April flood

of greenery and shine.
A colleague I despise
has brought his freshmen class outside.

Gathered like goslings at his feet,
some nod. Some pick at grass. Wind flips
the unread pages of their books.

It's poetry, I overhear him say,
the spirit's ancient longing voice. A pure
expression of the human soul.

He's all hogwash and hot air.
But even in the blossom-softened trees
the cardinals and the mockingbirds declare

it's just that kind of day, for song,
for saying something generous or grand,
or at the very least not small.

And Jesus, Anderson, what's wrong
with that? Besides, his students tend
to like him more than yours like you.

I wonder when that started being true,
or rather when it started meaning less.
Like tufted white chiffon,

clouds cruise the stained-glass blue Ohio sky,
and in the golden, post-
meridian decline of afternoon,

groundskeepers weed and mow. To them
we're just two lucky bastards who
teach twice a week then take the summers off.

Surely we must be chums.
Fat chance. No shot in hell. And yet
these days it gets more difficult to find

reasons to not be kind.
The bitchy, shrill remarks and self-regard
harder to justify.

Aprils are fewer now. Perhaps that's why.
Or maybe I just finally understand
silence and letting be are better things.

I should be better at them than I am.

Almost

The man behind me seethed.
                                        The lady behind him
kept sighing, clicking her high heel on cold
linoleum, and scowling at her watch.
The checkout boy was making change—*Snap! Snap!*—
one dollar at a time. He popped
each bill between his chubby fingertips,
glanced two times at the till, then smoothed
his singles, fives, and tens down on the countertop.
Each time: *Snap! Snap!* Glance twice and smooth.
The line was long and getting longer.
Two guys in John Deere hats showed up.
A mother and her infant. *Good gawd,*
I heard somebody say. *For crying out loud, kid.*
One woman slapped a pack of frozen peas
against her cheek. The line
was getting longer. A plumber. A cop.
Three busty girls with magazines and Diet Cokes.
Did his mother have any children that lived?
The man behind me laughed. The lady
just kept clicking her high heel.
                                        What happened next?
I set my basket on the belt.
I said, *It's Rodney, right?*
He thumbed his name tag. He nodded yes.
Hey Rodney, let's get out of here.

Forget these jerks. Forget this crappy job.
I tried to coax him out the way one might coax
a bashful, beaten dog to come.
                    It's just a job, I said.
I may even have whispered this.
C'mon. It's just a job. He looked at me
as if he didn't understand. *It's just a job.*
And he refused at first.
                    All I could hear
was someone cracking gum. Light music
overhead. The *click-click-clicking* of a heel.
We'll find you something else.
After a lengthy pause, he scanned
those fierce, exasperated faces in the line,
then finally he agreed.
Someone clapped. Another whooped, *Hell yes!*
And *Praise-the-fuh-cking-LORD!*
                    He closed
the register, stripped off his smock, then we,
we stepped out into seventy degrees.
Viburnum bloomed and honeysuckle bloomed.
Young parents strolled their baby down the street
and kids played Wiffle ball.
                    A frail, teetering man
clipped rhododendron blossoms from a bush.
On my front porch, Rodney sipped ginger ale.
I drank fine, caramel-colored bourbon on the rocks.
It's just, he started to say then stopped.
A cheerful *bird! bird! bird!* insistence sprang
throughout the leafy branches of my oaks.
It's just, I didn't want to disappoint my dad.

I almost called him "son." I almost said,
Your dad, who surely loves you very much,
will understand.
                                        I almost—*almost*—cupped
a gentle hand across his shoulder as he wept.
Except. Except he didn't weep.
He started ringing up my things,
then Rodney told me what I owed.
He bagged my tonic water and my chips,
and he, before he counted back my change,
apologized. *It's just this thing I have to do.*
Walking to my car, I only heard
the chiming clapper of a welcome bell, the sound
of gravel crunching underneath my feet.

In Vino Veritas

Over sliced apples and a wheel of cheese,
pale crescent moons of honeydew,
and three plump, golden loaves of bread,

we lift our glasses, lean them into light,
and each of us, as through
a jeweler's loupe, admires

the ruby and balsamic hue,
or something in between
garnet and tourmaline distilled

into a rich molasses brown.
Chocolate, someone muses.
Michigan cherries and a kiss of sage.

Tobacco and the slightest ghost
of clove. There is a lull until
the fellow next to me identifies

cracked pepper, orange zest,
blackberry, and vanilla bean.
Though not to be outdone,

another says these grapes
were punished early by the cold and wet
then rescued through a long

and providential miracle of sun.
Who wouldn't want to call to mind
a similar heroic year?

Or recount, with a dreamy look,
the way one woman does,
a weekend at this very same chateau,

the vintner's ancient Saint Bernard,
his fetching, broken English, and his wife's
delectable coquilles St. Jacques?

It gets so boring anymore,
listening to others tell you what they know
then somehow having to respond

as if you truly cared.
And yet, who can afford
in proper company

to say the other things out loud?
In the two decades we've been friends,
I've never really liked you very much.

Occasionally, I have
imagined having sex with Maxwell's wife.
Or this: *All snowy afternoon*

I've been uncomfortably aware
that everyone I know will someday die.
It's early still. I don't suppose,

if I slipped out to walk
the frozen, quiet quarter mile home,
that anyone would notice, much less care.

But surely I'll discern (I often do)
after latching the door and deadbolt lock,
a different kind of quiet waiting there.

Here, there is laughter, talk
of berries ripened on their summer vine,
the elemental taste

of husky fruit, of mineral and time.
Two conversations over, I can hear
Maxwell's intrepid voice grind on

about our taxes and the goddamned poor
when three mole-colored silhouettes appear—
two yearlings and a doe.

Their huge and darkly almond eyes!
Half curious, half terrified, they freeze
among the cedars, looking in.

And for the moment it's enough
to even make old Maxwell shut his yap—
three silent creatures on the silent snow,

those peach and lightly rose-pink evening clouds,
and fastened like an antique pin
above the cedars, also looking in,

a giant pearl apostrophe of moon.

From Here to There

She's talking to herself,
the woman on the subway next to me,
maybe it's someone else who isn't there,
a sister or a thankless child,
the husband I can't see.
Her tones are serious and low.
And though I can't make out the words,
the who or when or why,
whatever's being said, it isn't good
and seems to fluctuate
between apology and blame.
Commuting into darkness, side by side,
our tintype negatives appear
on the graffiti-etched
and grease-streaked window of the train.
We jolt and whip and chuck along
at dumb, erratic speeds.
In all that racket, it's clear,
she is, in fact, addressing *me.*
My narcissism, *my* ingratitude.
Past Chambers and Canal,
my petty jealousies
and endless list of thwarted plans.
Through 8th and 23rd and Herald Square,
all my colossal failures as a friend.
At one time or another, you must know,

you've disappointed each of us.
Just shy of 42nd she relents.
It's not entirely your fault, of course.
The way things were. Perhaps
this really is the best you could have done.
A hiss of brakes. The cry
of metal wheels on metal rails. And this
is 57th Street,
where I will rise, shuffle-step, and elbow out,
negotiating as I go
past an exhausted nurse,
the quiet waiter nuzzled in his book,
and a disheveled Wall Street broker
who has just pulled out a can of beer.
I climb into the nimble, bright
midtown Manhattan afternoon.
I'm relatively sure I comprehend
what loneliness and sorrow are,
but they've traveled further off,
to Forest Hills, North Riverdale,
Astoria, Jamaica Queens, or back
to desolated Sheepshead Bay.
The walk up 7th Avenue is brief
and Central Park, exploding into leaf,
is wealthy with the alternating airs
of fresh, hot sugar-roasted nuts,
loose hay, and carriage horse.
One seldom feels so ruthlessly alive.
Remember this: crocus and daffodil.
Old flannel men at chess. The robin-song.

A busy smear of taxis gliding by.
And studiously looking on,
washed in an otherworldly shine,
those stately, tall, impossible hotels.

Epithalamion in a Minor Key

Having caught him in a slight
and thoroughly inconsequential lie,
we watched him turn from us and wade
into a small, elegant cartel
of women beneath a water oak,
where he now smokes a cigarette alone.
The evening has the glazed and calm
enameled look of ornamental eggs.
Tree branches are laced with paper lanterns
and necklaces of tiny, ivory lights.
Filled water goblets gleam. The bride-to-be,
wearing a lemon cocktail dress and pearls,
seems chiseled from the very sun.
We know few people here
and find ourselves in conversation
with a gas and oil man from Baton Rouge,
two groomsmen, and the shy, well-meaning priest,
a surgeon from Rhode Island, and then
we're somehow milling next to *him* again.
He'd like to clarify
a certain thing he may have said before.
We wave it off. *Don't be absurd.*
This weekend all our causes are benign.
We mingle. We manage to avoid
opinion and belief.
Conservative and liberal. Hawk and dove.

Big Ten and SEC. No one
so far as I can tell
is giving anybody grief
over abortion or Afghanistan,
gay marriage or the Fed.
We're overly solicitous instead,
accommodating and sarcasm-free.
Nobody scoffs or cracks the sneer
that says, *You poor uneducated schmuck,*
you've swallowed all the propaganda, eh?
Miraculously, we
find only pleasantries to say
about the long distances we've come
and the "picture-perfect" weather.
We praise this rented stone estate,
its columns, the Italian marble stairs
and dazzling, cut-glass chandelier.
We remark how smitten they both look—
the almost bride and nearly groom
we're here to celebrate.
Tomorrow in the stained-glass chapel light,
wood polish and the pepper scent
of lilies hanging in the godly air,
a few may cry. A few
may privately suppose
there are no happy endings waiting there.
Someone will screw around, or worse,
someone will have to watch the other die.
To see them, though, so pleased,
so poised, so dashing, and so overjoyed,
it isn't difficult to think

these just may be the seldom two
who'll never raise their voices in a rage
or covet some lost solitude,
whose gentle, healthy children will obey,
whose mild hearts may, on occasion, drift
(as even mild hearts will sometimes do)
though never truly stray.
After the psalm and organ-driven hymns,
after the homily, the vows, that kiss,
wishing them happiness, if nothing else,
we wish them all of this.

At Advent's End

In icy Sunday morning light
my neighbor hauls her Christmas to the curb:
a snow-flocked noble fir,
armloads of garland, and a tinseled wreath.
These sag and flatten underneath
three pregnant garbage bags
of liquor bottles, boxes, cookie tins,
crushed wrapping paper, ribbon, bows,
and nubs of candles spiced
with cinnamon, apple, and pine.
They've gone: the Wise Men and the infant Christ,
Mary and Joseph, too,
who had been congregating there
in freezing rain and recent sleet
under her spot-lit ornamental pear.
She labors to remove
the mint and crimson window lights
that sparkled on our dark December street.
At last she hustles out and flings
a shriveled, little fist of mistletoe
on top of all that *was*,
then swivels, leans, and spills a whole
bright batch of popcorn from a metal bowl
for pigeons huddled on a wire.
They fall in soft, gray cotton flatteries

and muffled claps of flight
when quietly spirits appear
of orphaned plans, good intentions, blue maps
of all the places that I didn't go.
The spent endowment of another year
and January brooding like a ship,
luxury berths and iced champagne,
confetti and a foghorn sending-off
awaiting all of us.
Toward what?
Sun-crested archipelagoes of hope.
I'll get more organized.
I'll be more punctual and self-possessed,
more grateful than I ever was.
Our chimneys breathe and sigh
at such a moment so immense.
Then out of nowhere comes
a toddler's cry of sirens ranging near
until the shrieking blast
of city paramedics diesels past,
scattering pigeons in a gust of noise
and leaving in its wake
only the silver shake
of sleigh bells being taken from a door.
Our houses once again
are disappointed, sad, and plain.
Inside, where restlessness and boredom grow,
the days are shorter than they seem.
Some pace the carpet, others play at cards.
Some hunker down beside the fire.

In second-story rooms,
cluttered with disregarded toys and clothes,
stir-crazy children pray for snow.

II

This First Hot Saturday in May

The plump, governing bees
discover our tomato blooms,
our squash and watermelon blooms.
They tickle, kiss, and plumb
the open, velvet flower heads
of iris and hibiscus blooms.
They levitate and drift
among the purple hanging clouds
of blossoming wisteria.
This first hot Saturday of May,
the doused and dripping garden smells of green.
The catbird and electric finch,
the feisty jay and oriole
nip thistle, millet, milo seed, and corn
from feeders I have filled.
The world has come alive
with energy and appetite
and all the grand astonishments of sex.
It used to be the only thing
I ever thought about.
Cleavage. Athletic legs.
Tan lines, tight jeans, and lacy bras.
Now it's the nest egg and the ass at work,
a water heater that's about to blow,
election politics, and how
it feels the globe is going all to hell.

This would have seemed miraculous if not
entirely impossible to me
a quarter century ago.
What do the young expect?
I guarantee it isn't this:
a mortgage and a morning picking weeds,
the pleasurable shade
and savory tobacco scent of mulch.
Our fig tree and our lemon tree
survived an April frost.
Now they relax in clear, gold light,
and this, I confess, this brings me joy,
but more than joy it brings
a thankfulness that I'm no longer young,
uncertain, and obsessed.
Besides, it isn't youth I want.
Who needs the grudges and the big ideas?
The idiot decisions and the hurt?
It isn't youth I want,
only the high, luxuriating sense,
beneath these excellent and clean
procrastinations of the sun,
that certain days—*this one*—
may never end.

A Late Apology

It was all ours, we joked.
A shambled, overgrown estate.
Hackberry trees, wisteria like rope,
the carport and the morning glory–choked
old flowerbed. All ours:
wild clumps of poison oak, a lank,
rust-eaten corrugated shed,
shattered and whole clay pots,
an overwhelming, ripe chaos of weeds.
All ours: wood roach and bottle fly,
hornet and wasp, sweat bee,
the blue skinks and the millipedes,
and leering like a wasted, bloodshot eye,
a red-hot marble spider
clenched at the center of her web.
I can't forget, larger than my
two human arms around,
her supple, taut, and silken net,
or how three moist, green mornings in a row
we marveled over everything she caught:
dew-glistened crickets, clumsy moths,
and phosphorescent lightning bugs.
But what I can't remember now
is why or even how
our words that summer's night turned cross.

Dead certain I was right
(though who could say whatever I
was right about?), I slammed
one door. I let another bang behind
then smoldered slightly out of range,
just far enough where I might still hear
a reconciling call.
But no call ever came,
only the minor, iron cries
of passing Alabama trains.
It was a shallow, touchless night of sleep,
troubled by wind outside,
white thunder cracks and hammer-hissing rains,
but when we woke the world was fresh,
cornflower-pale and clear.

That's been nearly a year.
Sometimes I can still see it flutter there—
a tattered, ghostly, broken web
like floss or silver wisps of widow's hair
tickling the morning air
as if it were a thing that might be said
of sorrow or regret.
But standing in that ochre dawn
I chose a different thought instead,
making a vague remark
about the weather's sudden, gorgeous change
and all our gaudy myrtle blooms
that swayed and dandled overhead.

Provinces

Moon-glow projections on a screen reveal
    a drunken row of huts.
It's difficult to tell if those are goats
    or just emaciated cows
grazing at weeds among some hay carts.
    It is a chiseled, godforsaken place.
Unmapped. Ambiguous. Potato-beige.
    Nothing glints. Nothing sparkles.
Not one thing nourishes the eye.
    But lately, on the hamlet's western edge,
there have been strange movements—
    convoys of trucks arriving after dark.
The construction of a generator shed.
    An ever-slight increase
in local population.
    To get there would require,
for one of these distinguished, graying men,
    light packing and a taxi ride,
the shuttle up to JFK,
    a change of flights in Frankfurt, then
another eighteen hours over land.
    Ice paddles in a water-filled carafe.
Someone has brought in pastries on a tray.
    A pewter-blue light bathes
this undersecretary and his staff,
    who must consider what it means

now that reliable informants say
        the silo and the splintered barn conceal
a weapons cache and drums of surplus fuel.
        Within three days the village well,
that laundry drying on the line,
        the smokehouse, and the school
will lie in calculated heaps
        of bloody rags and planks, while you or I
watch college football on TV
        or bitch that it's been weeks
since we've had any decent rain.
        It's true. The purples and magentas drain
from our hydrangeas, and the lawn
        is August-straw and parched.
Our fig trees and magnolias weep
        from nearly seven years of drought.
Each night we track the surging cost
        of gasoline, the market's steep,
inconceivable decline.
        The polar ice caps melt.
The seas' green waters warm and rise.
        It is a dull, protracted age
of worry, ambiguity, and doubt,
        and yet the neighbor boys play otherwise,
who, armed with plastic M16s, patrol
        the pruned, bird-busy hedges, where
three others twitter, shush themselves, and wait.
        Crouching like fedayeen,
they rest their rifle barrels on a gate,
        and when they open fire

their girlish laughter nearly drowns
        the clack-clack-clacking of their guns.
But there are also other sounds:
        wind chimes. A hammer somewhere whacking nails.
The sighing of a passing car.
        Our small tomato garden goes to seed.
Reading her magazine, my wife enjoys
        the tender blessings of the evening sun,
and everything seems kissed
        with coral, gold, and lime.
Thank God, I sometimes think though never say,
        that *this* is where we are.

Teaching *The Merchant of Venice*

They reek of alcohol and sweat,
my Thursday morning students
who proclaim, *It's party week!*
It's only eight a.m.
                                        Imagine my dismay.
Is it so goddamn easy to forget,
an inner voice inquires,
that you would have been hungover, too,
bloodshot (if even here at all,
you self-righteous jerk!),
daydreaming about intercourse,
longing for bed and leering out
on those soft, golden cello notes of sun,
the mustard-yellow maples,
and the misty mid-October air?
Fine. So I blunder on
about the play's sundry problems:
Antonio's ennui,
these ruthless Christians, and the squeamish co-
existence of the comic and the cruel,
etcetera, etcetera.
They bear it with a patient shrug.
Not thirty minutes in
I see it shining there—act three, scene one—
ever so slightly coiled,
a strand of Susan Kelley's chestnut hair.

It is her Shakespeare after all,
or rather *was* until
she graduated, packed her life,
left me her books and 10-speed bike,
then shipped to Africa for mission work.

Outside, the glossy autumn morning grows
cantankerous with several squabbling crows.
Their fracas punctuates
the drowsy, leaden silences in here.
We'll write, we told ourselves.
We'll call. Two years from now
we'll pick up just where we left off.
Things seldom end so well.
Hilarious Toledo girl. Blue-eyed,
briefly imagined college bride
who figured that I wouldn't understand
the loneliness, the stress, the other boy.
They planned, not then exactly, but in time,
to be engaged.
She cried a little, then was gone.
When she apologized, it's true,
I didn't understand.

Forgive me, Susan Kelley, for the stunned
and sulky undergraduate I was.
I've certainly forgiven you
wherever you are now,
where it is surely apple season, too,
if not homecoming week,
when all our ghosts of being young are born.

These sophomores fidget in their seats.
Their pens make curlicues,
fishnets, primitive huts, flowers in fields.
Bassanio, Portia, Tubal, Shylock, all
are waiting in another room
where LOVE and JUSTICE doubt
that any of us ever gets it right.

I'd like to look her up sometime,
not out of jealousy
or lust or anything like spite,
but maybe just to have a laugh,
to say I found this strand of your brown hair,
etcetera, etcetera. And by the way,
I went to Venice once.
I saw the white Rialto,
the great basilica,
and the Piazza San Marco.
I stood a while and gazed
into those questionably green,
unsavory waters of the Grand Canal.
It was autumn. The light
was quite magnificent—a bluish gold.
I know that it's been years,
and this is anybody's guess, but still
I think you'd like it there.

The Hills, Beautiful Hills

The attic still smells of boredom,
sawdust, mothballs, and the rain
I climbed up here to watch
decades ago as it congealed
softly into Sunday snow.

I've come again to lose myself
among these stale, outdated clothes,
bad landscape paintings,
a stern dressmaker's dummy, and a fox—
the rusty, eyeless stole that guards it all:

framed needlepoints, mismatched crutches,
a paper sack of agates,
and postcards: Niagara Falls,
Mount Rushmore, and the Hoover Dam.
Or this one here in which

an ice-green Chrysler glides
through autumn in New England.
The woods are writhing and alive,
emphatic with persimmon hues,
with nectarine and plum.

But in the old Dutch Masters boxes,
these Packs and mackerel Satterfields
and all these silver-splashed DeMints

suggest an age of mercury,
magnesium, and lead.

In living rooms the color of trout,
in low-slung kitchens stained
with cigarette and iron-skillet smoke,
on rickety porches looking out
across magnetic Appalachian fields,

my disappointed, coy, and awkward kin
seem always caught distracted
on some lonely lane of thought,
and bothered into smiling
when they would rather not.

It's easier to love them now—
Aunt Bernadette and her afflicted son,
our Brylcremed uncle and his second wife,
the snowy-headed, feeble few
whose bedsides reeked of vapor rub and tea,

and all these tarnished dead I never knew:
canasta players, servicemen,
a graduating class of nurses,
and this barefooted, nameless girl who walks
her nickel-eyed emaciated hound.

Listen. You can nearly hear
the moist and muffled static sound
of a half-tuned radio,
but it's just the rain on the roof
that drowns the rowdy laughter down below,

the cackle, tease, and boast
of cousins on a raw November day
who, having warmed themselves with wine,
will shortly feast
on simmered apples, yeast rolls, and a roast.

How pleased and mild he looks here,
our granddad Claude,
relaxing in the old savannah swing
in what must be his sixty-sixth
or sixty-seventh year.

His days, they say, grew deeper
into silence, darker into doubt.
Was it the child they lost in '17?
The two world wars in which
he never fought? The heart attack?

Was it the prison term
that no one ever talks about?
His charcoal sweater zippered to the chin,
he lets the clear, thin light of early spring
rinse over him.

Meanwhile those West Virginia hills
behind him roll away, diminishing
like love or memory
or even loss,
in galvanized percentages of gray.

Insomnia at Forty-Six

Hours like these
we sit here in the satisfying dark.
Wind whistles at the chimney cap.
A bird's-eye maple clock keeps cadence,
knock by hollow, polished knock.

Though she's been dead ten years,
mother and I explain ourselves.
Together, we admire the blue
reversals of the mantle mirror,
the catlike quiet of our street,

and her antique mahogany buffet.
Hours like these there seems so much,
yet even we both know
there is little left to say.
My mother, who was never very young

or happy or at ease, and I agree:
our history seems ever slight
beneath each cold, unshattered, far-flung star—
Antares, Castor, Vega, Acamar—
that crackles in the midnight overhead.

I prefer to think I would know how
to love her many sorrows better now,

and she suspects that's true.
Hours like these
the disapproving boy I was still sees

her raging, inward, long debates,
those fixed, bewildered eyes and pinch-purse lips,
the subtle tremor of her head.
What were you saying, mother? And to whom?
and what, in turn, from that strange other room,

was also being said?

Easter Sundays

These yellow April evenings I,
no longer idealistic or inclined
to wish my life were something that it's not,
sip gin and tonics and enjoy
a fragrant breath of just-mown grass.
Immaculately laned front lawns
are flower-crowned, our windows bright and clean.
The lime wedge bobbing in my glass
suggests an effervescent, new,
and utterly surprising thought of green.
Who could complain? Yet someone surely will,
about the pollen count or lack of rain.
Not me. No one is happier than I
to watch the sprinkler's grainy rainbow spill
across broad vacancies of watered light
or study sun-glazed copper weathervanes
stamped against the cloud-flown April sky.

But still, it happens nearly every spring—
a blossomed stroll through Holy week,
Good Friday off, a lull, and then
that sadness Easter Sundays always bring.
It's hard saying exactly why.
It's not as if I even got to church,
though there are those who wish I would.

Why isn't it enough just being good?
Extending charity, I mean,
kindness, compassion, concern, and love?
All things I like to *think* I do.
Who needs an organist and choir,
a brass collection plate, the priest,
and an excruciating pew? Truth is,
it's something that I've often understood:
a deep desire to believe and belong.
Communion in a stony, cool,
and solemn atmosphere. Women
who dress and smell like fresh-cut flowers.
Men starched and ironed, splashed with aftershave.
The comfort *someone's* looking after us.
That kind of reassurance has a price—
worship with purpose, prayer on time,
ice-cream socials, driving kids to camp,
reading to shut-ins, selling Christmas wreathes.
It's not enough, just being nice,
and I suppose I understand this, too.

But what about the ones who get it wrong,
who do all this and still despise
the stupid and the ugly and the poor?
Perhaps they celebrated God in song,
tithed 10 percent and kneeled to pray,
but then two-timed the marriage, harbored hate
against their neighbors, screwed a friend or two—
not even really anything that's *new.*
It's just so dull. You'd think they'd preach

a little less, not judge so much.
But who am I to say? It's just so dull,
that righteous indignation of the blessed.

My next-door neighbor hates my guts,
at least when we talk politics he does.
He loves me like a brother, though,
when we talk gardening, cooking, music, dogs.
We plan long weekend trips we'll never take—
wine country or the coast. Our families eat
together once a week or more.
This isn't paradise, I know.
This isn't paradise, it's only home.
And yet imperfect as it is,
it would be difficult to disagree,
another Easter days away,
that home seems just about as flawless now
as it may ever be.

III

Labor Day

Beneath this blunt
and dusky colored onion light,
flounder glint like wet cobblestones
or dismal, rainy lakes.
Mackerel and amberjack,
exasperated cod, salmon, and trout—
gill-deep in diamond heaps of ice—
possess the heirloom sheen
of tarnished candlesticks, thimbles,
and old unpolished spoons.
Yet here and there,
far more exquisite alchemies persist.
A peacock-blue aluminum
articulates a basket of sardines.
Bronze and copper lusters gild the chub.
These freshly fallen nickel pickerel scales
seem rinsed in iridescent hues
of lavender and jade.
His thoughts are otherwhere and far,
the monger who relaxes
and gazes out
into the oyster-gray
and damp, coin-driven day.
His drizzle-misted window frames
the clownish colors
of a fruit and flower stand

across Third Avenue.
Tulip and orange-bright.
Apple and lily. Yellow rose and grape.
There are no optimists in here,
only these jelly-eyed,
distracted, sad inhabitants of doubt—
mackerel and amberjack,
exasperated cod,
flounder, and disbelieving trout—
who, though disgruntled, also seem resigned
to these lukewarm September easy rains
and this cool, humid air,
a sea-moist, tacky atmosphere
in which the evanescent tastes
of longing and departure blend.
And you, whoever you may be,
might well detect them too:
a mild salt breeze. Vacated cottages.
A padlocked clam shack and the closed café.
Those lapping, lightly gasolined
green harbor waters
at summer's still, lonely end.

The Novelist to His Characters

> All people, nations, and languages, trembled and
> feared before him: whom he would he slew;
> and whom he would he kept alive.
>
> DANIEL 5:9

Relax. Grow comfortable inside your skin.
Take solace. Everything will go as planned.
The wicked shall impose their will. The innocent
shall die because they must, you know. The cancer death
and late affair were both predestined long ago.
Your themes—what else?—are mortality and love.
But all your cruel particulars are mine.
The child's stutter. A cousin's palsied hand.
One's paralyzing phobia of beards. The twitch,
long speculated on though never quite explained,
of Great Aunt Esther, widowed by The War.
I've labored to perfect your flaws and fears,
the secret scars that one day will illuminate
your greed and inexplicable maliciousness.
Your thirsts, your predatory skills and calumnies
have germinated from a lush ancestral seed,
or possibly some prepubescent shame—
a playground gaffe or a bully's prank at your expense
that you'll remember mostly when you breathe the smell
of cafeteria soups or certain cleansers.
Bow down before this troubling dream.
Take solace, though, in knowing it will end.
Your chief antagonist will spend

eternity alone, arrested in the throes
of his advancing age. Incontinent and frail,
he'll loiter on that final page,
and glower out the window on his second floor,
surveying fields of snow, the cutleries of ice,
bare bodkins gleaming in the February sun.
Your names. Your names may chime a bell.
But mainly he'll recall one August as a boy.
First kiss. His uncle's modest, clapboard country house.
Blackberry gathering at dusk. This is his hell:
an endless afternoon beside a dying fire.
The cup of hot tea steaming just beyond his grasp.
An antique hunting rifle mounted on the wall.

Someone Is Burning Leaves

This season I admire most,
this season I sometimes obsess about,
goes up in muted, gorgeous flame.
Hornbeam and leatherwood, locust and larch,
the frosty lacebark elm
and mountain silver bell combust
in pumpkin color and the gold of corn.
Somewhere, someone is burning leaves,
and evening is weighted with a taste
of hickory and steel,
with leaf meal and the coolness of decay.
We've found each other after all this time.
Somebody said he'd died.
Another said she thought he'd been in prison.
But Jeffrey Day is very much alive.
Not only that, he's never spent
a single night in jail.
He calls me on the weekends in the fall,
most times more than a little drunk.
He had two houses and a boat,
a Jet Ski and a kick-ass pickup truck.
A couple DUIs and, *shit,*
he's lost it, lost it all.
But Jeffrey Day could play some ball!
he often interjects.

A speedy, lean, wasp-waisted kid
through peewee and in junior high,
a standout wide receiver senior year,
and then a freshman season on the squad
at Long Beach State. But now his hands
are like fat slabs of country ham,
nicked up from carpentry and warehouse work.
He's blown his back, his ankles, and his knees.
He hunches and he lumbers when he walks.
That's right. The boy could play some ball!
Mid-sentence I can hear
the puncture and the carbonated spray
of long-lost Jeffrey Day
cracking another can of beer.
We love you, Danny Anderson.
Now, we're not gay or anything like that,
it's just, we love you, baby, you be safe.

One recess during lunch,
this must have been the sixth or seventh grade,
I watched him saunter up
and cold-cock Kenny Ambrose in the mouth.
No reason whatsoever. *Smack!*
And Kenny Ambrose never said a word.
He didn't even cry.
He just looked horrified—at me, at first,
then Jeffrey Day and back at me again.
Remember that! Jeff jabbed
his finger straight at Kenny's face
before he pivoted then skipped away.

That childhood we survived
diminishes with every year
and smells this very night
like someone somewhere burning leaves.
The cellar prospers now
with onion, apple, parsnip, beet, and yam.
The cupboards bulge with canning jars
of stewed tomatoes, cucumbers, and beans.
Remember that! I do.
Exhausted garden flowers singe and brown,
and somewhere to the north, the crisping north,
a river's water blackens in the cold.
Yes, Jeffrey Day, we love you, too.

Four Voices for the Afterlife

i.m. M.M. (April 4, 1960–November 13, 1993)

Which time she chanted snatches of old lauds,
As one incapable of her distress.

HAMLET, 4.7

NOVEMBER 15, 1993

When she comes to you
still clenched, terrified, and sad,
escort our sister to a small salon,
a hearth-lit, crackling den
where maple logs unlock their supple blue
and mesmerizing copper light.
Give her a blanket, as soft as mink,
a satin pillow
for our weary sister's head.
And may she only hear
that little trickling sound of fire.

Because you have no right words
for loneliness and sorrow there,
because all that has happened
cannot be undone,
persuade our parents' daughter not to speak.
Instead, delight her as they did
when she was pink and young,
with a glaze of fresh orange

on her suckling lips,
the buttery and golden weight
of honey on their daughter's tongue.

Ringlet of waterdrop. Sweet flowerfold
of steam. After a hot, gray-vapored bath,
bring her lemon-yellow towels, a robe
as white as morning milk. Perfume
that chamber for our brother's resting wife
with lavender and clove, the good,
clean scent of pear. Each night,
light candles on her windowsill.
reacquaint her with a deep,
oxygen-inebriated sleep,
that slumber our rambunctious nephews know,
her puzzled sons, who spent
this umber Monday afternoon
marauding in the yard,
and who, just now, have come indoors,
their faces cold and raw,
smelling of stone and soil and early snow.

September 6, 1994

We see her sometimes in our dreams.
She is impossible as pollywogs
to snatch, or swallowtails.
Our mother teases us
at freeze-tag, hide-and-seek, and prisoner's base.
Bobwhite! Waxwing! Whippoorwill! Crow!
Who will catch me when I go?
She is impossible to snatch

as skinks or damselflies.
We see her sometimes in our dreams,
do you? A weeping woman who
has lost her boys. We *are* your boys,
we always say. Then mother
stops her weeping, wipes her eyes,
and walks away. School started yesterday
and we, we were her brave young men,
as clean, she liked to say, as whistles, washed
and combed, obedient, polite. We rode
our beastly yellow rumble-bus.
We greeted Mrs. Wilhelm
at the schoolhouse door.
And then, inside, they came again—
those stomach-churning, sweet
odors of floor wax, lunchroom food,
and finger paint. On Saturdays
she used to make French toast,
dusty with powdered sugar, soaked
in maple syrup. Now,
our father cooks us cream of wheat instead.

January 7, 1996

Ours is an old, embarrassing cliché.
Tea lights. Martinis on the rocks.
Two out-of-towners in a lounge
whose friendly chitchat somehow led
to innuendo, then
advances of a kind that cause

a self-respecting soul to wince.
And eight years later, here it is,
her ivory, wallet-softened business card
among these ballpoint pens,
a random champagne cork,
odd matchbooks, and a small confetti pile
of Chinese fortunes in my office drawer.
Things happen, as they say.
An elevator ride. The light
gardenia scent of her perfume.
Lobe. Lip. And a lover's breath.
That awkward after-silence, then a cheap
and punctual remorse. Once in a while,
I wonder what she thinks of me.
Henry, our fat black
barrel-chested Labrador,
still tuckered from his morning run,
absorbs a picture window spill of sun,
and like a silver bell,
my wife's bright laughter rings the whole house through.
A dishpan clatters in the kitchen, where
our robed and slippered daughters
clamor for breakfast and a fire.
The rich and rising smell
of bacon wakes the Sunday morning air.
What more could anyone desire?

August 11, 2001

You haven't smoked in years and yet,
after the cocktails and the Côtes du Rhône,
an utterly superb
and gratifying tenderloin,
grilled peaches, sautéed corn,
and mango-lime sorbet, you crave
the toasted flavor of a cigarette,
when, summoned like a ghost,
invisible to everyone but you,
a girl named Martha McEnroe appears,
tomboyish, muscular, and lean,
black braids and bangs,
those glacial, lake-blue Siamese eyes,
as daunting as she ever was
in tenth-grade English class.
Your host, who's pouring coffee, offers cream,
a slight enamel bowl of sugar cubes.
Perhaps another splash of Port?
You've always wondered why
or when, at least, it started going wrong,
but mostly you remember
a gorgeous, boring night not unlike this,
the summer after junior year, that high
electric throbbing song
of katydids, a rare cool snap,
and several of you gathered in a field.
Even now you can see
that moon-drenched little group
whose conversation doesn't matter,

but rather this: the glowing, cherry nib
of Martha's Camel Light, and how
for twenty fumbling minutes in the dark
her tongue and lips tasted
of nicotine and beer.
More than anything, you'd like to ask
if Martha ever thought about that night,
though she is nowhere now
and you—*Good Lord*—are nearly forty-two,
largely content with your concerns:
a decent if unsatisfying job,
your local school board,
and the recent undulations of the Dow.
Sometimes you tell yourself
you may have seen it stirring even then,
though then it seemed indifference or ennui,
a kind of melancholy, lonely pose.
She's no one anyone would know.
And who could even understand? You feel
the cool familiar pressure of a hand.
Your wife asks if you'd like to go.
Then Martha disappears
into the drowsy, floral-scented dark,
a lilting summer nothingness,
where she will spend the intervening years
until she calls again,
not uninvited, merely unannounced,
like green heat lightning in an August cloud
or the freshened April air
after the rain.

Mare Cognitum

The Windsor knot is loose.
At last, the number-driven mind
relaxes in its race, and he begins
the drowsy, dull commute
out to the leafy suburbs in the east.
Talk radio or Brahms or just
the leather cockpit quiet of his car,
it's only incidental noise behind
an undulating chain
of ruby brake lights traveling home
on the Interstate.
Six exits left to go
before the turn up Gladys Avenue,
the shopping traffic near the mall,
a roundabout, and then the right that veers
him past the elementary school,
a firehouse, and the nursing home.
His is the driveway next to mine.
Evenings, when he arrives,
we often mark the brief
and easy intersection of our lives
with enthusiastic waves,
sometimes a shout.

Tonight, the moon is whole.
It rises custard-yellow and immense

over our roofs and fat magnolias.
He strides from his garage. He bellows out,
Hey! Get a load a that!
Together in the moment we
take measure of what's looming there.
Abandoned planet. Ice-impacted place.
Those countrysides embossed
with moguls, powder-sunken lakes, and frost.

Before they got divorced,
we listened to them fighting every night.
Doors and cupboards slammed. Wine glasses shattered.
At least it seemed like every night.
Most weekends now he gets his boys.
They help him wash and wax the car.
All three of them rake leaves. They play catch.
Whoever dreams that love might come to this?
How rapidly that moon,
in its phosphorous and lonely climb,
diminishes to a medallion size.
It blanches plaster-white!
The moon, no doubt,
—our bright, unblinking winter eye—
must see this happen all the time.

Now: A Benediction

Three record-breaking weeks of heat.
Three weeks of waking up
unrested, angry, and drenched with sweat.
Three weeks when every midnight noise
was amplified and even more shrill—
sirens and car alarms,
huge dumpster-banging garbage trucks,
the howls of whiskey-pickled drunks
who couldn't—*could not*—stop themselves
from yelling, yelling, yelling
about how freaking hot, hot, hot it was.
Do you remember this?
For three oppressive weeks
that antique oscillating fan
and window unit wheezed.
Three weeks, and we consumed iced everything.
Iced coffee and iced tea. Ice cream.
Chilled gin martinis shaken over ice.
For twenty days, the morning news
and evening news announced another day
of record-crushing heat.
Queer, radiating waves
shimmered and warped above our streets.
The broad and flabby leaves of sycamores
snapped at their stems, shriveled, and fell.
Remember this? We argued even then

because, we told ourselves,
people who loved each other did that, too.
We raged and blamed, we pacified, made peace
and then made love (a phrase we both detest).
Eventually, we raged and blamed again.
At lunch, some days, I sat whole hours
in shade beside a fountain where
a bawdy Neptune bathed
among his chiseled, stocky water gods.
Whole hours, the spatter, slap, and prance
of thunder-gush and shower drowned—
then cooled—whatever passed for hurt,
whatever may have even passed for hate.
On my way home, I sometimes stopped
for irises, for oranges, for wine.
All that anybody talked about
was three obsessive, brutal weeks
of suffering, of punishment.
Remember, though, that there was laughter, too.
Laughter and tenderness. Laughter and light.
And, yes, laughter and love.

Today, these sudden whipping gusts
lift towels and bed sheets drying on the lines.
The rising, cold-front wrath of wind
knocks over folding chairs and potted plants.
And now, the sterling silver weight of rain.
Mad coins—nickels and dimes—pummel the roof,
the windows, streets, and fire escapes.
Gutter and culvert flood.
Let there be greenery again,

shy mushrooms, mold rosettes,
blossoming colonies of rust.
Let our exhausted, ruthless world
seem limitless once more,
replenished, one more time,
and possible again,
for each of us, and just.

Acknowledgments

I would like to thank the editors of the following magazines in which some of these poems first appeared.

Birmingham Poetry Review: "Almost," "At Advent's End," "Someone Is Burning Leaves."

Cincinnati Review: "From Here to There."

Hopkins Review: "Epithalamion in a Minor Key," "Four Voices for the Afterlife," "In Vino Veritas," "Labor Day," "Teaching *The Merchant of Venice.*"

The Journal: "Mare Cognitum."

Missouri Review: "The Hills, Beautiful Hills," "Pardon and Amnesty," "Provinces."

New Madrid: "The Novelist to His Characters."

Northwest Review: "A Late Apology," "The Night Guard at the Wilberforce Hotel."

Subtropics: "Easter Sundays," "This First Hot Saturday in May."

Yale Review: "Insomnia at Forty-Six."

While there are many people who make my life uniquely blessed, I would especially like to express my gratitude to Phil Borack, Claudia Fladung, Heather Levy, Candace Gordon, Sharon Bandy, Buzz Sienknecht, Andrew Hudgins, Erin McGraw, Barbara and Wyatt Prunty, Woody Register, and Christine Schutt for their generosity and bountiful care.

And again, thanks to John Irwin, my editor.

About the Author

Daniel Anderson is the author of two collections of poetry—*Drunk in Sunlight* (2006) and *January Rain* (1997)—and the editor of Howard Nemerov's *Selected Poems.* He has held teaching positions at Murray State University, the University of the South, Kenyon College, the University of North Carolina, and the University of Alabama at Birmingham. Currently, Anderson is an associate professor at the University of Oregon, where he teaches in the graduate creative writing program.

Poetry Titles in the Series

John Hollander, *Blue Wine and Other Poems*
Robert Pack, *Waking to My Name: New and Selected Poems*
Philip Dacey, *The Boy under the Bed*
Wyatt Prunty, *The Times Between*
Barry Spacks, *Spacks Street: New and Selected Poems*
Gibbons Ruark, *Keeping Company*
David St. John, *Hush*
Wyatt Prunty, *What Women Know, What Men Believe*
Adrien Stoutenberg, *Land of Superior Mirages: New and Selected Poems*
John Hollander, *In Time and Place*
Charles Martin, *Steal the Bacon*
John Bricuth, *The Heisenberg Variations*
Tom Disch, *Yes, Let's: New and Selected Poems*
Wyatt Prunty, *Balance as Belief*
Tom Disch, *Dark Verses and Light*
Thomas Carper, *Fiddle Lane*
Emily Grosholz, *Eden*
X. J. Kennedy, *Dark Horses: New Poems*
Wyatt Prunty, *The Run of the House*
Robert Phillips, *Breakdown Lane*
Vicki Hearne, *The Parts of Light*
Timothy Steele, *The Color Wheel*
Josephine Jacobsen, *In the Crevice of Time: New and Collected Poems*
Thomas Carper, *From Nature*
John Burt, *Work without Hope: Poetry by John Burt*
Charles Martin, *What the Darkness Proposes: Poems*
Wyatt Prunty, *Since the Noon Mail Stopped*
William Jay Smith, *The World below the Window: Poems 1937–1997*
Wyatt Prunty, *Unarmed and Dangerous: New and Selected Poems*
Robert Phillips, *Spinach Days*
X. J. Kennedy, *The Lords of Misrule: Poems 1992–2001*
John T. Irwin, ed., *Words Brushed by Music: Twenty-Five Years of the Johns Hopkins Poetry Series*
John Bricuth, *As Long As It's Big: A Narrative Poem*
Robert Phillips, *Circumstances Beyond Our Control: Poems*
Daniel Anderson, *Drunk in Sunlight*
X. J. Kennedy, *In a Prominent Bar in Secaucus: New and Selected Poems, 1955–2007*
William Jay Smith, *Words by the Water*
Wyatt Prunty, *The Lover's Guide to Trapping*
Charles Martin, *Signs & Wonders*
Peter Filkins, *The View We're Granted*
Brian Swann, *In Late Light*
Daniel Anderson, *The Night Guard at the Wilberforce Hotel*

CPSIA information can be obtained at www.ICGtesting.com
Printed in the USA
LVOW11s0909240316

480564LV00003B/155/P

9 781421 413471